Valleys

by Sheila Anderson

first step nonfiction

Lerner Publications Company · Minneapolis

What is a **valley?**

It is a kind of **landform.**

A valley is a piece of land
between hills or mountains.

A valley is lower than the
land beside it.

Some valleys are dug
by rivers.

These valleys are shaped
like the letter *V*.

Some valleys are made
by **glaciers.**

These valleys are shaped
like the letter *U*.

Valleys can be dry and dusty.

Valleys can be green.

Animals live in valleys.

Plants grow in valleys.

People live in valleys.

People grow **crops** in valleys.

There are many things to
do in a valley.

Would you like to explore a valley?

Glaciers

A glacier is like a river made of ice. Glaciers form high in mountains and in very cold places. Glaciers are made of snow that has turned to ice. Glaciers move very slowly. They pick up dirt and rocks as they move along. Some glaciers move toward the ocean. When the ice in a glacier reaches the ocean, it breaks off and floats away. Some glaciers do not reach the ocean. They melt and form lakes.

Valley Facts

 Valleys with very steep sides are called canyons or gorges.

 One of the most famous canyons is the Grand Canyon. It is located in Arizona. The Colorado River has carved the canyon over millions of years.

 People travel from all over the world to see the Grand Canyon. They hike down into the canyon. People even ride donkeys down into the canyon to explore.

Another famous valley in the United States is Death Valley. It is located in California.

 In the summer, the average high temperature in Death Valley is over 105° Fahrenheit (40.56° Celsius), and the average low is about 80° Fahrenheit (26.67° Celsius).

 The highest temperature recorded in Death Valley was 134° Fahrenheit (56.67° Celsius).

Glossary

 crops – plants people grow to use for food or other purposes

 glaciers – a large piece of ice that moves slowly down a mountain or through a valley

 landform – a natural feature of the earth's surface

 valley – a long, narrow area of land between mountains or hills

Index

animals – 12, 20

glaciers – 8, 19

hills – 4

mountains – 4

people – 14, 15, 16, 20

plants – 13, 15

rivers – 6, 19, 20

The photographs in this book are used with the permission of: © Gavin Hellier/Robert Harding World Imagery/Getty Images, pp. 2, 22 (bottom); © Bill Heinsohn/Photographer's Choice/ Getty Images, pp. 3, 22 (second from bottom); © Melissa McManus/Stone/Getty Images, p. 4; © Steve Razzetti/Taxi/Getty Images, p. 5; © Philippe Colombi/Stockbyte/Getty Images, p. 6; © Keren Su/China Span/Getty Images, p. 7; © Arctic Images/Iconica/Getty Images pp. 8, 18, 22 (second from top); © Panoramic Images/Getty Images, p. 9; Eitan Simanor/Taxi/Getty Images, p. 10; © Toby Maudsley/Iconica/Getty Images, p. 11; © Eliot Elisofan/Time & Life Pictures/ Getty Images, p. 12; © Michelle Garrett/Red Cover/Getty Images, p. 13; © Walter Bibikow/ Riser/Getty Images, p. 14; © Michael Buselle/Stone/Getty Images, pp. 15, 22 (top); © Brian Bailey/Riser/Getty Images, p. 16; ©Jochen Schlenker/Robert Harding World Imagery/Getty Images, p. 17.

Front Cover: © John Wang/Digital Vision/ Getty Images.

Lerner Publications Company
A division of Lerner Publishing Group, Inc.
241 First Avenue North
Minneapolis, MN 55401 U.S.A.

Website address: www.lernerbooks.com

Library of Congress Cataloging-in-Publication Data

Anderson, Sheila.
    Valleys / by Sheila Anderson.
        p.   cm. — (First step nonfiction. Landforms)
    Includes index.
    ISBN: 978–0–8225–8591–6 (lib. bdg. : alk. paper)
    1. Valleys—Juvenile literature. 2. Valley ecology—Juvenile literature. I. Title.
GB561.A53 2008
551.44'2—dc22   2007007823

Manufactured in the United States of America
1 2 3 4 5 6 – DP – 13 12 11 10 09 08